MW01491007

Carb Cycling

A simple guide with Delicious Recipes to Burn Fat and Build Strong Muscle

By

Dr. Tate Mandara

Copyright © 2024 by Dr. Tate Mandara

Table of Contents

INTRODUCTION

Carb cycling is a dietary strategy that has been widely used in fitness and bodybuilding communities for decades. Originally, athletes and bodybuilders adopted this approach to optimize performance and maintain a lean physique. The concept revolves around alternating between high-carb and low-carb days to fuel workouts, enhance fat loss, and regulate hormones such as insulin. Over time, carb cycling gained popularity outside the athletic world, as people discovered its benefits for weight management, improved energy levels, and better metabolic health.

For men over 50, carb cycling is particularly beneficial. As men age, they often experience a decrease in muscle mass, a slower metabolism, and increased fat storage. Carb cycling helps to balance hormones, improve insulin sensitivity, and promote fat loss while preserving muscle mass. This approach offers a flexible, sustainable way to manage weight and enhance overall health, making it a valuable tool for those looking to optimize their nutrition as they age.

Anthony Milton, a 54-year-old businessman, faced typical struggles for his age: weight gain, chronic fatigue, and declining muscle mass.

As his career became more demanding, his health began to take a backseat. He felt powerless over his expanding waistline and low energy levels. Then, Anthony discovered this carb cycling. By following a structured carb cycling plan, he could tailor his nutrition to his body's needs, fueling himself with carbs on active days and reducing them on rest days. The results were life-changing. Within a few months, he lost over 10 pounds, regained muscle tone, and saw a marked improvement in his energy levels. His fatigue dissipated, and his confidence returned. This book offers the same life-altering strategy that helped Anthony, designed specifically for men over 50 to combat similar health challenges.

CHAPTER ONE

Overview of Carb Cycling

Carb cycling is a dietary strategy that involves alternating between high-carb, low-carb, and sometimes no-carb days, depending on your activity levels, goals, and body's needs. For men over 50, this approach becomes especially relevant as the body's metabolism, hormone levels, and muscle mass begin to shift due to aging.

The core idea of carb cycling is to strategically time your carbohydrate intake to support energy needs, enhance fat loss, and promote muscle maintenance. On high-carb days, you consume more carbohydrates to fuel intense workouts, replenish glycogen stores, and support muscle repair. On low-carb or no-carb days, the body relies more on fat for energy, promoting fat burning and improving insulin sensitivity.

For men over 50, carb cycling is not only about managing weight but also adapting to the body's changing needs. As testosterone and growth hormone levels decrease with age, it becomes harder to maintain muscle mass and easier to gain fat.

Carb cycling helps combat this by providing the right fuel at the right time, allowing older men to maintain muscle and avoid unwanted fat gain.

The process involves careful planning of meals, ensuring that high-carb days coincide with more active or strength training days, while low-carb days align with rest or lighter activity. Protein intake remains consistent throughout, ensuring muscle preservation, while fat intake varies depending on carb intake.

This dietary method allows men over 50 to adjust their carbohydrate intake according to their fitness goals and lifestyle, helping them stay energized, build lean muscle, and manage weight effectively as they age. Unlike one-size-fits-all diets, carb cycling offers flexibility and personalization, making it a sustainable option for long-term health.

Benefits of Carb Cycling for Men in Their 50s and Beyond

Promotes Fat Loss: Carb cycling helps the body burn fat more effectively by reducing carbohydrate intake on low-carb days, encouraging the body to use fat as its primary energy source.

Maintains Lean Muscle Mass: By timing carb intake around workouts, men in their 50s can maintain and even build muscle, despite the natural decline in testosterone and growth hormone levels with age.

Improves Insulin Sensitivity: Low-carb and no-carb days enhance the body's ability to regulate blood sugar and insulin, reducing the risk of insulin resistance, which becomes more common as men age.

Boosts Energy and Performance: High-carb days provide the necessary fuel for intense physical activities, ensuring better performance during workouts and quicker recovery after strenuous exercise.

Supports Hormonal Balance: Carb cycling can help balance hormones, such as testosterone and cortisol, which can be disrupted as men age. The cycling of carbs ensures that the body is neither deprived of energy nor overloaded, which can stress hormone levels.

Enhances Mental Clarity: On low-carb days, some men experience improved cognitive function and mental sharpness, as the body burns fat for energy, producing ketones, which are efficient fuel for the brain.

Increases Metabolic Flexibility: Carb cycling helps the body adapt to using both carbohydrates and fat for energy, keeping the metabolism active and reducing the risk of metabolic slow-down.

Prevents Dietary Fatigue: The flexibility of alternating between carb intake levels keeps the diet dynamic, preventing boredom and improving long-term adherence.

The Science Behind Carb Cycling and Aging

As men age, their bodies undergo significant changes that affect metabolism, hormone levels, and muscle mass. Carb cycling offers a tailored approach to these changes, helping men over 50 manage their weight, maintain energy, and preserve muscle. By adjusting carbohydrate intake, carb cycling can combat the effects of aging while promoting overall health and longevity.

Metabolic Slowdown & Hormonal Changes

One of the major challenges men face as they age is a slowing metabolism. Around the age of 50, testosterone levels begin to decline, which can lead to increased body fat and decreased muscle mass. Alongside this, growth hormone production drops, further contributing to metabolic slowdown. Carb cycling helps counter this by providing higher carbohydrates on active days to fuel energy and lower carbohydrates on rest days to encourage fat burning. This alternation keeps the metabolism active and prevents it from becoming sluggish.

Hormonal changes also include increased levels of cortisol, a stress hormone that can lead to fat storage, particularly around the abdomen. Carb cycling, by offering the right balance of nutrients, helps stabilize cortisol levels while maintaining healthy energy and hormonal balance.

Insulin Sensitivity and Blood Sugar Control

As insulin sensitivity decreases with age, the body becomes less efficient at processing carbohydrates, leading to higher blood sugar levels and increased risk of insulin resistance. Carb cycling addresses this by incorporating low-carb or no-carb days that help improve insulin sensitivity. When combined with exercise, carb cycling can regulate blood sugar levels, reducing the risk of type 2 diabetes and other metabolic disorders. This strategy ensures that the body remains efficient at managing blood glucose.

Importance of Preserving Muscle Mass

Maintaining muscle mass is crucial as men age, not only for physical strength but also for metabolic health. Muscle is more metabolically active than fat, meaning the more muscle you have, the more calories you burn at rest. Carb cycling provides the necessary fuel on high-carb days to support muscle-building workouts while promoting fat loss on low-carb days. This dual approach allows men in their 50s and beyond to preserve and even enhance their muscle mass while preventing the decline in strength and mobility that often accompanies aging.

By addressing these key aspects of aging, carb cycling becomes an effective dietary approach for men over 50, helping them stay healthy, active, and fit.

CHAPTER TWO

Fundamentals of Carb Cycling

Learn how this method, tailored for men over 50, can balance energy levels, support muscle maintenance, and enhance general health, all while adapting to your unique needs and lifestyle.

Structuring Your Carb Cycling Plan

Creating an effective carb cycling plan is essential for achieving optimal results, especially for men over 50 who are looking to manage their weight, energy levels, and muscle mass. By strategically alternating between high, low, and no-carb days, you can tailor your nutrition to meet your body's changing needs, helping you feel energized and fit.

How to Design a Weekly Cycle (High, Low, and No/Very Low Carb Days)

A standard carb cycling plan typically consists of three types of days: high-carb, low-carb, and no/very low-carb days. On high-carb days, which are often paired with intense workouts, you consume more carbohydrates to fuel energy and support muscle recovery. For example, high-carb days may include 50-60% of your calories coming from carbs. These days help replenish glycogen stores and provide energy for your workouts. Low-carb days, typically scheduled on lighter workout or rest days, involve reducing your carb intake to around 20-30% of your daily calories. These days encourage fat burning while still providing enough carbs for basic functions.

No or very low-carb days are usually reserved for complete rest days, where carbs are kept under 10% of your daily intake. This phase promotes fat burning and can enhance ketosis, a state where the body uses fat as its primary energy source.

Customizing Based on Activity Levels

When designing your carb cycling plan, it's important to tailor it to your individual activity levels. On days when you have more intense physical activity, like strength training or cardio sessions, you should increase your carb intake to fuel performance. Conversely, on less active or rest days, reduce carbs to encourage fat loss. Customizing your carb intake based on your workouts ensures that you're always providing your body with the right fuel at the right time, making your carb cycling plan more effective and sustainable.

Macronutrient Ratios for Men Over 50

As men age, their bodies undergo metabolic changes that require careful consideration of macronutrient ratios to maintain optimal health. Balancing carbs, proteins, and fats becomes especially important for men over 50 to preserve muscle mass, manage energy levels, and support overall well-being. Adjusting these macronutrients appropriately can help combat age-related challenges like muscle loss and slowed metabolism.

Adjusting Carbs, Proteins, and Fats

For men over 50, adjusting the intake of carbohydrates, proteins, and fats can significantly impact health and fitness outcomes.

Carbohydrates should be adjusted based on activity levels. On high-carb days, around 50-60% of total calories should come from carbs to fuel performance and energy. On low-carb days, aim for about 20-30% carbs, and on no-carb days, less than 10% to encourage fat burning and support metabolic health.

Fats play a crucial role in hormone regulation, especially testosterone, which naturally declines with age. Healthy fats should make up around 20-30% of total caloric intake, providing necessary nutrients while supporting overall vitality.

Proteins are essential for muscle preservation, and for men over 50, protein intake should remain high, contributing around 30-40% of total calories. Protein supports muscle recovery, reduces muscle loss, and keeps metabolism strong as you age.

Importance of Protein Intake for Muscle Preservation

Protein is particularly vital for men over 50, as it helps combat sarcopenia (the natural loss of muscle mass due to aging). Maintaining or increasing protein intake ensures that muscles have the necessary building blocks to repair and grow after physical activity. Protein also aids in controlling appetite, stabilizing blood sugar levels, and boosting metabolism. Consuming lean sources of protein like chicken, fish, eggs, and plant-based options is key to supporting muscle mass and overall health in the later years of life.

Timing Meals Around Activity for Men Over 50

Properly timing meals around physical activity is key to maximizing the benefits of carb cycling for men over 50. As your body undergoes changes due to aging, aligning carb intake with exercise and structuring your daily meals can help boost energy, support muscle preservation, and enhance fat burning. Timing your nutrition correctly can make all the difference in reaching your fitness and health goals.

How to Match Carb Intake with Exercise

Carb intake should be carefully matched with physical activity to optimize performance and recovery. On high-carb days, consume a larger portion of your carbohydrates around your workouts. This ensures that you have enough glycogen stores to fuel your exercise, whether it's strength training, cardio, or endurance activities. For men over 50, consuming carbs before and after workouts can help maintain energy levels during exercise and promote muscle recovery afterward.

On low-carb days, your carb intake will be reduced, so focus on lighter activities like walking, yoga, or stretching. These activities do not require as much energy from glycogen stores, making it easier to rely on fat for fuel. Prioritize healthy fats and proteins during these days to support muscle maintenance and energy balance.

Best Time of Day for High and Low Carb Consumption

The timing of carb consumption is also essential for men over 50. On high-carb days, it's best to consume most of your carbs earlier in the day, such as around breakfast and lunch. This helps provide energy for the day's activities and gives your body enough time to use the carbs efficiently. Having carbs around your workout windows, typically during the mid-morning or early afternoon, will also enhance performance.

On low-carb days, focus on eating the bulk of your carbs earlier in the day, but keep it minimal. Save your low-carb, high-fat, and protein-rich meals for dinner, as this will help stabilize blood sugar levels and promote fat burning overnight, which is crucial for overall metabolic health as you age.

CHAPTER THREE

Carb Cycling Phases

High Carb Days (Fueling Performance)

Harness the power of high-carb days to boost energy and improve athletic performance. Learn how strategically timed carbohydrates enhance endurance, support recovery, and optimize your workouts effectively.

Benefits of High Carb Days for Men Over 50

Boosting Energy and Enhancing Exercise Performance: High carb days are essential for men over 50 to maintain optimal energy levels and enhance exercise performance. As we age, our energy needs can fluctuate, and high-carb days help to meet these increased demands. Carbohydrates are the body's primary source of fuel, particularly for high-intensity activities. By incorporating high-carb days into your regimen, you provide your muscles and liver with an ample supply of glucose, which is crucial for sustained energy during workouts.

This increased energy not only helps you to exercise more effectively but also contributes to better overall physical performance.

Replenishing Glycogen Stores: After periods of low-carb intake, the body's glycogen stores can become depleted. Glycogen, stored in muscles and the liver, is a vital source of energy for physical activity. High carb days are strategically placed to replenish these stores, ensuring that your body has adequate reserves for subsequent workouts. This replenishment is especially important for older adults, as maintaining optimal glycogen levels supports endurance and reduces fatigue. Efficient glycogen storage also aids in preventing muscle breakdown and promoting quicker recovery from exercise.

Supporting Muscle Growth and Repair: For men over 50, maintaining muscle mass and supporting recovery is crucial. High-carb days play a significant role in muscle growth and repair by providing the necessary energy for protein synthesis. Carbohydrates stimulate insulin release, which helps in the uptake of amino acids into muscle cells. This process is essential for muscle repair and growth.

Additionally, having adequate glycogen stores ensures that muscles are not depleted of energy during workouts, further supporting their recovery and growth. Integrating high-carb days into your diet plan can thus enhance muscle maintenance and overall fitness.

What to Eat on High Carb Days

Best Sources of Healthy Carbohydrates (Whole Grains, Starches, Fruits): On high carb days, it's important to focus on nutrient-dense sources of carbohydrates to fuel your body effectively and support overall health. Whole grains are an excellent choice, offering sustained energy and essential nutrients. Examples include quinoa, brown rice, oats, and barley. These grains provide fiber, which aids in digestion and helps maintain stable blood sugar levels. Starches, such as sweet potatoes, butternut squash, and legumes, are also valuable. They are rich in complex carbohydrates, which release energy slowly and prevent spikes in blood sugar. Fruits are another vital component, as they not only offer natural sugars but also provide vitamins, minerals, and antioxidants. Opt for fruits like berries, apples, bananas, and oranges to get a variety of nutrients while satisfying your carb needs.

Balancing Carbs with Proteins and Fats: While focusing on high-carb intake, balancing these carbs with adequate proteins and fats is essential for maintaining a well-rounded diet and ensuring overall health.

Proteins are crucial for muscle repair and growth, especially for men over 50. Incorporate lean proteins such as chicken breast, fish, tofu, and legumes into your meals. Healthy fats are also important for hormone production and overall cell function. Include sources like avocados, nuts, seeds, and olive oil in your diet. When planning your meals, aim to create balanced plates where carbohydrates, proteins, and fats complement each other. For instance, a meal could include grilled chicken (protein), quinoa (carb), and a side of roasted sweet potatoes (starch) with a drizzle of olive oil (fat). This balance helps in optimizing nutrient absorption and supports sustained energy levels throughout the day.

Low Carb Days (Promoting Fat Loss)

On low carb days, your body shifts to burning stored fat for energy. Learn how reducing carbs accelerates fat loss, supports weight management, and enhances metabolic health, especially for men over 50.

Benefits of Low Carb Days for Men Over 50

Enhancing Fat Burning and Weight Loss: Low carb days can significantly boost fat burning, which is particularly beneficial for men over 50. By reducing carbohydrate intake, the body is encouraged to use stored fat for energy, leading to more effective weight loss. This approach helps combat age-related metabolic slowdowns and can be a key strategy for achieving and maintaining a healthy weight.

Maintaining Stable Blood Sugar Levels: Low carb days contribute to better blood sugar control by minimizing insulin spikes and crashes. For men over 50, who may be more prone to insulin resistance, stable blood sugar levels are crucial for overall health. This approach helps manage energy levels throughout the day and reduces the risk of developing type 2 diabetes.

Balancing Hormones and Insulin Sensitivity: Reducing carb intake can positively impact hormone levels, particularly insulin. For older men, maintaining optimal insulin sensitivity is vital for metabolic health and reducing the risk of chronic conditions. Low carb days help in balancing hormones and improving the body's response to insulin, supporting long-term health and well-being.

What to Eat on Low Carb Days

Ideal Low-Carb Foods (Non-Starchy Vegetables, Healthy Fats, Lean Proteins): On low carb days, focus on incorporating foods that are low in carbohydrates but high in essential nutrients. Non-starchy vegetables such as spinach, kale, and bell peppers are excellent choices. These vegetables provide vital vitamins and minerals without adding excessive carbs. Healthy fats are also crucial; include avocados, olive oil, and nuts like almonds or walnuts, which support hormone production and overall health. Lean proteins, such as skinless chicken breast, fish, and tofu, help in muscle repair and maintenance. These foods not only fit well within a low-carb framework but also ensure you get a balanced intake of nutrients.

Nutrient-Dense Choices for Men Over 50: For men over 50, it's important to select nutrient-dense options that support aging bodies. Opt for fatty fish like salmon and mackerel, rich in omega-3 fatty acids, which are beneficial for heart health and cognitive function. Incorporate eggs and Greek yogurt for their high-quality protein and essential nutrients. Low-carb, high-fiber foods such as chia seeds and flaxseeds are excellent for digestive health and maintaining satiety. Focus on vegetables that are high in antioxidants, like broccoli and Brussels sprouts, to combat inflammation and oxidative stress. These choices help in maintaining energy levels, preserving muscle mass, and supporting overall well-being as you age.

No/Very Low Carb Days (Enhancing Ketosis & Insulin Sensitivity)

Discover how zero and very low carb days can drive your body into ketosis, improving insulin sensitivity, and maximizing fat burning for optimal metabolic health and energy balance.

The Power of No/Very Low Carb Days

Triggering Ketosis for Fat Burning: No-carb and very low-carb days are instrumental in triggering ketosis, a metabolic state where the body burns fat for energy instead of carbohydrates. By significantly reducing carb intake, the liver converts fatty acids into ketones, which serve as an alternative energy source. This shift helps in efficient fat burning, supporting weight management and reducing body fat percentage, particularly beneficial for men over 50 facing metabolic slowdowns.

Improving Insulin Sensitivity: Incorporating no or very low-carb days into your diet can enhance insulin sensitivity. Lower carbohydrate consumption decreases insulin spikes and levels, allowing the body to manage glucose more effectively. Improved insulin sensitivity reduces the risk of type 2 diabetes and helps stabilize blood sugar levels, which is crucial for metabolic health as we age.

Promoting Mental Clarity and Energy: Ketosis not only benefits physical health but also supports cognitive function. Many individuals report improved mental clarity and sustained energy levels during very low-carb periods. This is because ketones provide a steady energy supply to the brain, avoiding the energy crashes often associated with high-carb diets. Enhanced mental focus and reduced fatigue make these days highly effective for maintaining productivity and overall well-being.

How to Safely Implement No Carb or Very Low Carb Days

Adjusting for Men Over 50 with Medical Conditions: For men over 50, particularly those with medical conditions like diabetes or hypertension, implementing no-carb or very low-carb days requires careful planning. Begin by consulting your healthcare provider to tailor the approach to your specific health needs. Monitor blood sugar levels closely if you have diabetes, as drastic reductions in carbs can affect insulin requirements.

For hypertension, ensure that your diet includes adequate potassium and magnesium to balance electrolytes, as low-carb diets can sometimes lead to imbalances. Gradually adjust your carb intake to avoid sudden shifts that might cause discomfort or adverse effects.

Ensuring Adequate Nutrition on No Carb Days: On no-carb or very low-carb days, it's crucial to maintain a balanced intake of essential nutrients. Focus on consuming nutrient-dense foods like leafy greens, non-starchy vegetables, and high-quality proteins (such as lean meats, fish, and eggs). Incorporate healthy fats from sources like avocados, nuts, and olive oil to provide energy and support health. Be mindful to include a variety of foods to cover all vitamin and mineral needs. Consider supplementing with electrolytes, such as sodium, potassium, and magnesium, to avoid deficiencies that can arise from reduced carb intake. Proper planning ensures that you get the nutrients necessary to sustain health while reaping the benefits of a low-carb approach.

CHAPTER FOUR

Exercise Strategies for Carb Cycling

Optimize your carb cycling results with targeted exercise strategies. Combining the right workouts with your carb cycle enhances performance, supports muscle growth, and boosts metabolism. This chapter delves into effective exercise routines tailored for men over 50, helping you maximize the benefits of carb cycling.

Types of Exercise to Pair with High and Low Carb Days

Strength Training on High Carb Days: High-carb days are ideal for intense strength training. Carbohydrates provide the necessary energy and replenish glycogen stores, enhancing performance during workouts. Focus on compound movements like squats, deadlifts, and bench presses to build and maintain muscle mass. Aim for 3-4 sessions per week, incorporating progressive overload to challenge your muscles and stimulate growth. With the extra energy from high-carb days, you can push harder and recover faster, making these workouts more effective in building strength and muscle.

Cardio and Fat-Burning Exercises on Low Carb Days: On low-carb days, your body shifts to using fat as a primary fuel source, making it an optimal time for cardio and fat-burning exercises. Engage in moderate-intensity activities like brisk walking, cycling, or swimming, which can help maximize fat oxidation. Consider adding high-intensity interval training (HIIT) for efficient calorie burning and improved cardiovascular health. Keep cardio sessions around 30-45 minutes, ensuring they don't overly deplete your energy levels. This approach helps leverage the body's fat-burning mode while respecting the lower energy availability of low-carb days.

Combining these exercise strategies with carb cycling can enhance overall fitness, optimize muscle growth, and support effective fat loss, especially for men over 50.

Sample Weekly Workout Plan for Men Over 50

Matching Carb Intake with Activity Levels: A well-structured workout plan for men over 50 should align exercise intensity and type with the carb cycling schedule. Here's a sample weekly workout plan to maximize results:

Monday (High Carb Day): Focus on strength training with heavy compound exercises such as squats, deadlifts, and bench presses. Aim for 3-4 sets of 8-12 reps per exercise. The increased carbohydrate intake fuels these intense workouts and supports muscle growth and recovery.

Tuesday (Low Carb Day): Engage in moderate-intensity cardio like brisk walking or cycling for 30-45 minutes. The reduced carbs enhance fat utilization, making it a great day for burning fat while still keeping energy levels steady.

Wednesday (High Carb Day): Continue with strength training, focusing on different muscle groups or varying exercises from Monday's session. Incorporate accessory movements to target specific areas. This high-carb day ensures you have the energy for effective workouts and recovery.

Thursday (Low Carb Day): Perform a combination of light cardio and flexibility exercises, such as yoga or stretching. This helps maintain cardiovascular health and flexibility without overtaxing your system.

Friday (High Carb Day): Repeat strength training with a focus on different exercises or increasing weights. The extra carbs support another intense workout session, optimizing muscle gain and overall strength.

Saturday (Low Carb Day): Opt for low-impact activities like a leisurely walk or gentle swimming.

This helps in active recovery while keeping carbs low to enhance fat burning.

Sunday: Rest day. Allow your body to recover fully from the week's activities. Use this time for light stretching or gentle activities if desired.

Recovery and Rest Strategies: Recovery is crucial, especially for men over 50. Ensure 7-9 hours of quality sleep each night to aid muscle repair and overall health. Incorporate rest days strategically to prevent overtraining and reduce the risk of injury. Utilize techniques like foam rolling, stretching, and hydration to support muscle recovery and joint health. Adequate rest combined with a balanced workout plan and proper nutrition enhances overall well-being and performance.

CHAPTER FIVE

Adapting Carb Cycling for Medical Conditions

Adapting carb cycling for men over 50 with medical conditions requires careful planning. Tailoring the approach ensures it supports health needs while optimizing benefits. This chapter provides strategies to adjust carb cycling for diabetes, hypertension, and other conditions, ensuring a balanced and effective diet plan.

How Carb Cycling Can Be Tailored for Managing Medical Conditions

Carb cycling, when adapted for men over 50 with medical conditions, can be a powerful tool for managing health while achieving fitness goals.

For those with diabetes, a strategic approach is essential. High-carb days can be adjusted to include complex carbohydrates that have a lower glycemic index, helping to maintain stable blood sugar levels. Low-carb and no-carb days can be utilized to promote fat loss and improve insulin sensitivity, but must be monitored closely to avoid hypoglycemia.

For hypertension, focusing on a balanced intake of electrolytes is crucial. High-carb days can be paired with foods rich in potassium, magnesium, and calcium to support blood pressure regulation. On low-carb days, incorporating foods that are naturally low in sodium can help manage blood pressure without compromising the diet's effectiveness.

Cholesterol management benefits from the inclusion of heart-healthy fats and fiber. During high-carb days, opt for whole grains and fruits that are high in soluble fiber, which helps lower LDL cholesterol levels. On low-carb days, emphasize lean proteins and healthy fats like avocados and nuts, which support heart health while keeping cholesterol levels in check.

Tailoring carb cycling involves adjusting macronutrient ratios and food choices to meet specific health needs. Regular monitoring and consultation with your healthcare provider ensure that the carb cycling plan remains effective and safe, promoting overall well-being while managing medical conditions.

Addressing Joint Pain and Mobility Issues

For men over 50 experiencing joint pain and mobility issues, integrating anti-inflammatory foods and exercises into a carb cycling plan can provide significant relief and improve general function.

Anti-Inflammatory Foods: Incorporating foods that reduce inflammation is crucial for managing joint pain. Include omega-3-rich foods such as salmon, chia seeds, and walnuts, which help decrease inflammation and support joint health. Leafy greens like spinach and kale, along with berries, are high in antioxidants and can combat oxidative stress that contributes to joint pain. Turmeric and ginger are also effective due to their natural anti-inflammatory properties, and can be easily added to meals or smoothies.

Exercises: Gentle, low-impact exercises are beneficial for improving mobility without exacerbating joint pain. Swimming or water aerobics provides a full-body workout while reducing stress on the joints. Yoga and stretching exercises enhance flexibility and strength, and specific poses can target areas affected by arthritis or stiffness. For example, gentle stretching of the hips and lower back can relieve tension and improve range of motion. Resistance training with light weights or resistance bands can build muscle strength around the joints, offering better support and reducing pain. Combining these dietary and exercise strategies can help manage and alleviate joint pain, improve mobility, and support general health. It's essential to tailor both food choices and physical activities to individual needs and consult with your healthcare provider to ensure the approach is safe and effective.

Incorporating Supplements to Support Aging Bodies

As men age, their bodies undergo various changes that can benefit from targeted supplementation. Incorporating supplements into a diet plan can support general health, enhance energy levels, and improve specific age-related concerns.

Multivitamins: A high-quality multivitamin can fill nutritional gaps that may arise due to changes in dietary needs and absorption efficiency. Look for formulas that include essential vitamins like B12, D, and minerals such as magnesium and calcium, which are crucial for bone health and energy metabolism.

Omega-3 Fatty Acids: Supplements such as fish oil or algae-based omega-3s help reduce inflammation, support heart health, and improve cognitive function.

These are particularly beneficial as inflammation often increases with age.

Joint Support Supplements: Glucosamine and chondroitin can aid in maintaining joint health, reducing pain, and improving mobility. Turmeric and its active compound, curcumin, also offer anti-inflammatory benefits.

Protein Powders: For maintaining muscle mass, especially important as muscle loss accelerates with age, protein powders like whey or plant-based options can help meet protein needs.

Probiotics: These support gut health and improve digestion, which can be beneficial as digestive efficiency may decline with age.

Consult with your healthcare provider before starting any new supplement regimen to ensure they are appropriate for individual health needs and conditions.

CHAPTER SIX

HIGH-CARB BREAKFAST RECIPES

Overnight Oats with Banana and Honey

Serving: One
Preparation Time: 5 minutes (plus overnight soaking)
Cooking Time: 0 minutes

Ingredients:
- 1/2 cup rolled oats
- 1 cup almond milk
- 1 ripe banana, sliced
- 1 tablespoon honey
- 1 tablespoon chia seeds

Preparation Method:
1. In a jar or bowl, combine oats, almond milk, chia seeds, and honey.

2. Stir well and refrigerate overnight.

3. In the morning, top with sliced banana before serving.

Nutritional Value: Approximately 400 calories | 10g fat | 70g carbohydrates | 10g fiber | 20g sugar | 10g protein

Whole Wheat Pancakes with Maple Syrup

Serving: One
Preparation Time: 10 minutes
Cooking Time: 10 minutes

Ingredients:
- 1 cup whole wheat flour
- 2 tablespoons sugar (optional)
- 2 teaspoons baking powder
- 1/4 teaspoon salt
- 1 large egg
- 1 cup milk (dairy or non-dairy)
- 2 tablespoons maple syrup (for serving)

Preparation Method:

1. In a bowl, mix flour, sugar, baking powder, and salt.

2. In another bowl, whisk together milk and egg.

3. Combine wet and dry ingredients until just mixed.

4. Heat a skillet over medium heat and pour batter to form pancakes.

5. Cook until bubbles form; flip and cook until golden brown.

Nutritional Value: Approximately 350 calories | 8g fat | 60g carbohydrates | 4g fiber | 12g sugar | 10g protein

Whole Grain Pancakes with Banana

Serving: One
Preparation Time: 10 minutes
Cooking Time: 10 minutes

Ingredients:
- 1 cup whole grain flour
- 1 ripe banana, mashed
- 1 tablespoon honey or maple syrup
- 1 cup milk (dairy or non-dairy)
- 2 large eggs

Preparation Method:

1. In a bowl, combine flour, mashed banana, honey, milk, and eggs.

2. Mix until smooth.

3. Heat a skillet over medium heat and pour batter to form pancakes.

4. Cook until bubbles form; flip and cook until golden brown.

Nutritional Value: Approximately 400 calories | 9g fat | 70g carbohydrates | 5g fiber | 15g sugar | 12g protein

Quinoa Breakfast Bowl with Fruits

Serving: One
Preparation Time: 5 minutes
Cooking Time: 15 minutes (for quinoa)

Ingredients:
- 1/2 cup cooked quinoa
- 1/2 cup mixed fruits (berries, banana slices)
- 1/2 cup almond milk or yogurt
- 1 tablespoon honey or maple syrup (optional)

Preparation Method:

1. In a bowl, combine cooked quinoa and almond milk or yogurt.

2. Top with mixed fruits and drizzle with honey if desired.

Nutritional Value: Approximately 350 calories | 8g fat | 60g carbohydrates |5g fiber |20g sugar |12g protein

French Toast with Cinnamon Apples

Serving: One
Preparation Time: 10 minutes
Cooking Time:10 minutes

Ingredients:
• 2 slices whole grain bread
• 2 large eggs
• 1/4 cup milk (dairy or non-dairy)
• 1/4 teaspoon cinnamon
• 1 medium apple, sliced
• 1 tablespoon butter for cooking
• Optional toppings: maple syrup or powdered sugar

Preparation Method:

1. In a bowl, whisk together eggs, milk, and cinnamon.

2. Dip bread slices in the mixture to coat.

3. Cook in a skillet with melted butter until golden brown on both sides.

4. Sauté apple slices in the same skillet until tender; serve on top of French toast.

Nutritional Value: Approximately 450 calories |15g fat |65g carbohydrates |6g fiber|20g sugar|15g protein

LOW-CARB BREAKFAST RECIPES

Spinach and Goat Cheese Omelet

Serving: One
Preparation Time: 5 minutes
Cooking Time: 10 minutes

Ingredients:
- 3 large eggs
- 1 tablespoon heavy cream
- 1 cup fresh baby spinach
- 1 ounce goat cheese
- 1 tablespoon butter
- Salt and pepper to taste

Preparation Method:

1. In a bowl, whisk together eggs, heavy cream, salt, and pepper.

2. Heat butter in a non-stick skillet over medium heat.

3. Pour in the egg mixture and cook until edges start to set.

4. Add spinach and goat cheese to one side of the omelet.

5. Fold the omelet in half and cook for another minute until fully set.

Nutritional Value: Approximately 368 calories | 28g fat | 2g carbohydrates | 0g fiber | 1g sugar | 25g protein

Vegetable Scrambled Eggs

Serving: One
Preparation Time: 5 minutes
Cooking Time: 5 minutes

Ingredients:
- 2 large eggs
- 1/4 cup diced bell peppers
- 1/4 cup diced onions

- 1 tablespoon olive oil
- Salt and pepper to taste

Preparation Method:

1. Heat olive oil in a skillet over medium heat.

2. Add bell peppers and onions; sauté until soft.

3. Whisk eggs in a bowl, then pour into the skillet.

4. Stir gently until eggs are cooked through.

Nutritional Value: Approximately 250 calories | 20g fat | 4g carbohydrates | 1g fiber | 2g sugar | 12g protein

Low-Carb Breakfast Casserole

Serving: One
Preparation Time: 10 minutes
Cooking Time: 30 minutes

Ingredients:
- 4 large eggs
- 1 cup chopped spinach
- 1/2 cup diced bell peppers
- 1/2 cup shredded cheese (optional)
- Salt and pepper to taste

- 1 tablespoon olive oil

Preparation Method:

1. Preheat oven to 350°F (175°C).

2. In a skillet, heat olive oil and sauté spinach and bell peppers until soft.

3. In a bowl, whisk eggs, salt, and pepper; add sautéed vegetables.

4. Pour mixture into a greased baking dish and top with cheese if desired.

5. Bake for about 30 minutes or until set.

Nutritional Value: Approximately 300 calories | 20g fat | 6g carbohydrates | 2g fiber | 2g sugar | 20g protein

Smoked Salmon with Avocado

Serving: One
Preparation Time: 5 minutes
Cooking Time: None

Ingredients:

- 3 ounces smoked salmon
- 1/2 avocado, sliced
- 1 tablespoon cream cheese (optional)
- Capers or dill for garnish (optional)

Preparation Method:

1. Arrange smoked salmon on a plate.

2. Top with avocado slices and cream cheese if using.

3. Garnish with capers or dill if desired.

Nutritional Value: Approximately 300 calories | 20g fat | 8g carbohydrates |6g fiber|0g sugar|20g protein

Keto Avocado Toast

Serving: One
Preparation Time:5 minutes
Cooking Time: None

Ingredients:
- 1 slice low-carb bread
- 1/2 avocado
- Salt and pepper to taste

●**Optional toppings**: cherry tomatoes, radishes, or an egg

Preparation Method:

1. Toast the low-carb bread slice.

2. Mash avocado in a bowl; season with salt and pepper.

3. Spread mashed avocado on toast; add optional toppings if desired.

Nutritional Value: Approximately 250 calories |15g fat |10g carbohydrates |7g fiber|0g sugar|8g protein

HIGH-CARB LUNCH RECIPES

Quinoa and Black Bean Salad

Serving: One
Preparation Time: 10 minutes
Cooking Time: 20 minutes (for quinoa)

Ingredients:
●1/2 cup cooked quinoa

- 1/2 cup canned black beans, drained and rinsed
- 1/4 cup diced bell pepper
- 1/4 cup diced red onion
- 1/4 cup chopped cilantro
- 1 tablespoon lime juice
- 1 tablespoon olive oil

Preparation Method:

1. Cook quinoa according to package instructions and let it cool.

2. In a bowl, combine quinoa, black beans, bell pepper, red onion, and cilantro.

3. Drizzle with lime juice and olive oil; toss to combine.

Nutritional Value: Approximately 300 calories | 9g fat | 45g carbohydrates | 10g fiber | 2g sugar | 12g protein

Sweet Potato and Chickpea Bowl

Serving: One
Preparation Time: 10 minutes
Cooking Time: 25 minutes (for sweet potato)

Ingredients:
- 1 medium sweet potato, cubed

- 1/2 cup canned chickpeas, drained and rinsed
- 1 cup spinach
- 1 tablespoon olive oil
- Salt and pepper to taste

Preparation Method:

1. Preheat oven to 400°F (200°C).

2. Toss sweet potato cubes with olive oil, salt, and pepper; roast for about 20 minutes.

3. In a bowl, combine roasted sweet potatoes, chickpeas, and spinach.

Nutritional Value: Approximately 400 calories | 14g fat | 60g carbohydrates | 10g fiber | 5g sugar | 12g protein

Barley and Roasted Vegetable Soup

Serving: One
Preparation Time: 10 minutes
Cooking Time: 30 minutes

Ingredients:
- 1/2 cup cooked barley

- 1 cup mixed roasted vegetables (carrots, zucchini, bell peppers)
- 2 cups vegetable broth
- Salt and pepper to taste

Preparation Method:

1. In a pot, combine vegetable broth and roasted vegetables; bring to a simmer.

2. Add cooked barley; season with salt and pepper; heat through.

Nutritional Value: Approximately 350 calories | 5g fat | 70g carbohydrates | 12g fiber|6g sugar|12g protein

Lentil and Vegetable Stir-Fry

Serving: One
Preparation Time: 10 minutes
Cooking Time:15 minutes

Ingredients:
- 1/2 cup cooked lentils
- 1 cup mixed vegetables (broccoli, bell peppers, carrots)

- 1 tablespoon soy sauce
- 1 tablespoon olive oil

Preparation Method:

1. Heat olive oil in a skillet over medium heat; add mixed vegetables and sauté until tender.
2. Stir in cooked lentils and soy sauce; cook until heated through.

Nutritional Value: Approximately 300 calories |8g fat |45g carbohydrates |15g fiber|3g sugar|18g protein

Brown Rice and Grilled Chicken Bowl

Serving: One
Preparation Time:10 minutes
Cooking Time:20 minutes (for chicken)

Ingredients:
- 1/2 cup cooked brown rice
- 6 oz grilled chicken breast, sliced
- 1 cup steamed broccoli or green beans
- 1 tablespoon teriyaki sauce (optional)

Preparation Method:

1. Cook brown rice according to package instructions.

2. Grill chicken until fully cooked; slice.

3. Serve chicken over rice with steamed vegetables; drizzle with teriyaki sauce if desired.

Nutritional Value: Approximately 450 calories |10g fat |60g carbohydrates |8g fiber|5g sugar|40g protein

LOW-CARB LUNCH RECIPES

Scrambled Eggs & Veggies

Serving: One
Preparation Time: 5 minutes
Cooking Time: 5 minutes

Ingredients:
- 2 large eggs
- 1/2 cup mixed vegetables (spinach, bell peppers, tomatoes)
- 1 tablespoon butter or olive oil
- Salt and pepper to taste

Preparation Method:

1. Heat butter or olive oil in a skillet over medium heat.

2. Add mixed vegetables and sauté for about 3 minutes until tender.

3. Beat the eggs in a bowl, then pour into the skillet.

4. Stir gently until the eggs are fully cooked.

Nutritional Value: Approximately 250 calories | 20g fat | 4g carbohydrates | 1g fiber | 2g sugar | 12g protein

Low-Carb Chicken Parmesan

Serving: One
Preparation Time: 10 minutes
Cooking Time: 25 minutes

Ingredients:
- 4 oz boneless, skinless chicken breast
- 1/2 cup marinara sauce (sugar-free)
- 1/4 cup grated Parmesan cheese
- 1/4 cup shredded mozzarella cheese
- 1 tablespoon olive oil
- Salt and pepper to taste
- 1 teaspoon Italian seasoning

Preparation Method:

1. Preheat oven to 350°F (175°C).

2. Season chicken with salt, pepper, and Italian seasoning.

3. Heat olive oil in a skillet over medium heat; cook chicken for about 3-4 minutes on each side until golden.

4. Place chicken in a baking dish, top with marinara sauce and cheeses.

5. Bake for about 15 minutes until cheese is melted.

Nutritional Value: Approximately 400 calories | 22g fat | 6g carbohydrates |0g fiber|3g sugar|38g protein

Salmon Salad with Olive Oil

Serving: One
Preparation Time: 5 minutes
Cooking Time: None

Ingredients:
- 4 oz canned or cooked salmon
- 2 cups mixed greens (spinach, arugula, lettuce)
- 1/4 avocado, sliced
- 1 tablespoon olive oil

- Juice of half a lemon
- Salt and pepper to taste

Preparation Method:

1. In a bowl, combine mixed greens and salmon.

2. Top with avocado slices.

3. Drizzle with olive oil and lemon juice; season with salt and pepper.

Nutritional Value: Approximately 350 calories | 25g fat | 5g carbohydrates |5g fiber|0g sugar|30g protein

Broccoli and Cheese Frittata

Serving: One
Preparation Time: 5 minutes
Cooking Time: 15 minutes

Ingredients:
- 3 large eggs
- 1/2 cup chopped broccoli (fresh or frozen)
- 1/4 cup shredded cheddar cheese
- 1 tablespoon olive oil or butter
- Salt and pepper to taste

Preparation Method:

1. Preheat oven to broil.

2. Heat olive oil in an oven-safe skillet over medium heat; add broccoli and sauté for about 3 minutes.

3. In a bowl, whisk eggs and season with salt and pepper; pour over broccoli.

4. Cook until edges set, then sprinkle cheese on top and broil until cheese is melted and frittata is set.

Nutritional Value: Approximately 300 calories |22g fat |6g carbohydrates |2g fiber|2g sugar|20g protein

Steak Burrito Bowl

Serving: One
Preparation Time:10 minutes
Cooking Time:10 minutes

Ingredients:
- 4 oz grilled steak, sliced
- 1/2 cup cauliflower rice (or cooked brown rice if not strictly low-carb)
- 1/4 cup diced tomatoes
- 1/4 avocado, sliced

- 1 tablespoon salsa (optional)
- Salt and pepper to taste

Preparation Method:

1. In a bowl, layer cauliflower rice as the base.

2. Top with sliced steak, diced tomatoes, and avocado.

3. Add salsa if desired; season with salt and pepper.
Nutritional Value: Approximately 400 calories |25g fat |8g carbohydrates |5g fiber|0g sugar|30g protein

HIGH-CARB SNACK RECIPES

Oaty Apple Muffins

Serving: One
Preparation Time: 10 minutes
Cooking Time: 20 minutes

Ingredients:
- 1 cup rolled oats
- 1/2 cup applesauce
- 1/2 cup grated apple (about 1 small apple)
- 1/4 cup honey or maple syrup
- 1/2 teaspoon cinnamon

- 1 teaspoon baking powder
- 1/4 teaspoon salt

Preparation Method:

1. Preheat the oven to 350°F (175°C) and line a muffin tin with liners.

2. In a bowl, combine oats, applesauce, grated apple, honey, cinnamon, baking powder, and salt.

3. Mix until well combined and pour into muffin tins.

4. Bake for about 20 minutes or until a toothpick comes out clean.

Nutritional Value: Approximately 180 calories | 2g fat | 37g carbohydrates | 5g fiber | 12g sugar | 3g protein

Quinoa Energy Bites

Serving: One
Preparation Time: 10 minutes
Cooking Time: None (chill time required)

Ingredients:
- 1 cup cooked quinoa

- 1/2 cup rolled oats
- 1/2 cup almond butter
- 1/4 cup honey
- 1/4 cup ground flaxseed
- 1 teaspoon cinnamon

Preparation Method:

1. In a bowl, mix all ingredients until well combined.

2. Roll the mixture into balls (about the size of a tablespoon).

3. Place on a baking sheet and refrigerate for at least one hour to firm up.

Nutritional Value: Approximately 120 calories | 6g fat | 15g carbohydrates | 2g fiber | 7g sugar | 3g protein

Sweet Potato Chips

Serving: One
Preparation Time: 10 minutes
Cooking Time: 20 minutes

Ingredients:
- 1 medium sweet potato

- 1 tablespoon olive oil
- Salt to taste

Preparation Method:

1. Preheat the oven to 400°F (200°C).

2. Thinly slice the sweet potato using a mandoline or sharp knife.

3. Toss slices in olive oil and salt.

4. Arrange on a baking sheet and bake for about 20 minutes, flipping halfway through, until crispy.

Nutritional Value: Approximately 150 calories |5g fat |30g carbohydrates |4g fiber |5g sugar |3g protein

Hummus with Whole Grain Pita

Serving: One
Preparation Time:5 minutes
Cooking Time: None

Ingredients:
- 1/4 cup hummus
- 1 whole grain pita bread (about 60g)
- **Optional toppings**: paprika or olive oil for drizzling

Preparation Method:

1. Cut pita into triangles and serve with hummus for dipping.

Nutritional Value: Approximately 250 calories |8g fat |35g carbohydrates |6g fiber |0g sugar |8g protein

Whole Grain Crackers with Hummus

Serving: One
Preparation Time:5 minutes
Cooking Time: None

Ingredients:
- 10 whole grain crackers (about one serving)
- 1/4 cup hummus

Preparation Method:

1. Serve crackers with hummus as a dip.

Nutritional Value: Approximately 200 calories |8g fat |30g carbohydrates |4g fiber |0g sugar |6g protein

LOW-CARB SNACK RECIPES

Cucumber Slices with Guacamole

Serving: One
Preparation Time: 5 minutes
Cooking Time: None

Ingredients:
- 1 medium cucumber
- 1/2 avocado
- 1 tablespoon lime juice
- Salt and pepper to taste
- **Optional**: diced tomatoes or cilantro for garnish

Preparation Method:

1. Slice the cucumber into rounds and arrange them on a plate.

2. In a bowl, mash the avocado and mix in lime juice, salt, and pepper until smooth. Spoon the guacamole onto each cucumber slice.

3. Garnish with diced tomatoes or cilantro if desired.

Nutritional Value: Approximately 150 calories | 10g fat | 12g carbohydrates | 7g fiber | 1g sugar | 3g protein

Beef Jerky

Serving: One
Preparation Time: None (store-bought)
Cooking Time: None (store-bought)

Ingredients:
1 oz beef jerky (check for low-sugar varieties)

Preparation Method:

1. Simply open the package and enjoy as a snack.

Nutritional Value: Approximately 70 calories | 1g fat | 3g carbohydrates | 0g fiber | 1g sugar | 11g protein

Hard-Boiled Eggs with Avocado

Serving: One
Preparation Time: 10 minutes (for boiling eggs)
Cooking Time: None (if eggs are pre-boiled)

Ingredients:
• 2 hard-boiled eggs

- 1/2 avocado
- Salt and pepper to taste

Preparation Method:

1. If not pre-boiled, place eggs in a pot of water, bring to a boil, then simmer for about 9 minutes; cool and peel.

2. Slice the avocado and serve alongside or on top of the eggs.

3. Season with salt and pepper.

Nutritional Value: Approximately 320 calories | 24g fat | 6g carbohydrates | 5g fiber | 0g sugar | 18g protein

Cheese and Nut Plate

Serving: One
Preparation Time: 5 minutes
Cooking Time: None

Ingredients:
- 2 oz cheese (cheddar, mozzarella, or your choice)
- 1/4 cup mixed nuts (almonds, walnuts, pecans)

Preparation Method:

1. Arrange cheese slices and nuts on a plate; enjoy as a snack.

Nutritional Value: Approximately 400 calories | 35g fat | 10g carbohydrates |3g fiber|2g sugar|15g protein

Celery Sticks with Peanut Butter

Serving: One
Preparation Time: 5 minutes
Cooking Time: None

Ingredients:
- 2 large celery stalks
- 2 tablespoons natural peanut butter (no added sugar)

Preparation Method:

1. Cut celery stalks into manageable pieces.

2. Spread peanut butter into the grooves of each celery stick.

Nutritional Value: Approximately 200 calories |16g fat |8g carbohydrates |3g fiber|2g sugar|8g protein

HIGH-CARB DINNER RECIPES

Lentil Soup with Whole Grain Bread

Serving: One
Preparation Time: 10 minutes
Cooking Time: 30 minutes

Ingredients:
- 1/2 cup dried lentils
- 1/4 cup diced carrots
- 1/4 cup diced celery
- 1/4 cup diced onion
- 2 cups vegetable broth
- 1 slice whole grain bread
- Salt and pepper to taste

Preparation Method:

1. Rinse lentils and set aside.

2. In a pot, sauté onions, carrots, and celery until softened.

3. Add lentils and vegetable broth; bring to a boil.

4. Reduce heat and simmer for about 25 minutes until lentils are tender.

5. Season with salt and pepper; serve with whole grain bread.

Nutritional Value: Approximately 400 calories | 2g fat | 70g carbohydrates | 15g fiber | 5g sugar | 25g protein

Quinoa and Veggie Salad

Serving: One
Preparation Time: 10 minutes
Cooking Time: 15 minutes (for quinoa)

Ingredients:
- 1/2 cup cooked quinoa
- 1/4 cup diced cucumber
- 1/4 cup halved cherry tomatoes
- 1/4 cup diced bell pepper
- 1 tablespoon olive oil
- Juice of half a lemon

Preparation Method:

1. Cook quinoa according to package instructions; let cool.

2. In a bowl, combine cooked quinoa, cucumber, tomatoes, and bell pepper.

3. Drizzle with olive oil and lemon juice; toss to combine.

Nutritional Value: Approximately 300 calories | 10g fat | 45g carbohydrates | 8g fiber | 3g sugar | 10g protein

Bean, Pea, and Lentil Salad

Serving: One
Preparation Time: 10 minutes
Cooking Time: None (if using canned beans)

Ingredients:
- 1/4 cup canned black beans, rinsed
- 1/4 cup canned chickpeas, rinsed
- 1/4 cup green peas (fresh or frozen)
- 1/4 cup diced red onion
- 1 tablespoon olive oil
- Juice of half a lime
- Salt and pepper to taste

Preparation Method:

1. In a bowl, combine black beans, chickpeas, peas, and red onion.

2. Drizzle with olive oil and lime juice; season with salt and pepper.

3. Toss gently to mix well.

Nutritional Value: Approximately 350 calories |8g fat |60g carbohydrates |15g fiber |5g sugar |20g protein

Warm Lentil and Halloumi Salad

Serving: One
Preparation Time:10 minutes
Cooking Time:15 minutes

Ingredients:
- 1/2 cup cooked lentils
- 2 oz halloumi cheese, sliced
- 1 cup mixed greens (spinach, arugula)
- 1 tablespoon olive oil
- Salt and pepper to taste

Preparation Method:

1. In a skillet, heat olive oil over medium heat; add halloumi slices and cook until golden on both sides.

2. In a bowl, combine warm lentils with mixed greens; top with halloumi.

3. Season with salt and pepper before serving.

Nutritional Value: Approximately 450 calories |30g fat |30g carbohydrates |6g fiber |2g sugar |25g protein

Spinach, Lentil, and Feta Bruschetta

Serving: One
Preparation Time:5 minutes
Cooking Time:10 minutes

Ingredients:
- 2 slices whole grain bread
- 1/2 cup cooked lentils
- 1 cup fresh spinach
- 2 tablespoons crumbled feta cheese
- 1 tablespoon olive oil
- Salt and pepper to taste

Preparation Method:

1. Toast the whole grain bread slices until golden brown.

2. In a skillet, sauté spinach until wilted; mix in cooked lentils.

3. Top toasted bread with the lentil-spinach mixture and sprinkle with feta cheese; drizzle with olive oil.

Nutritional Value: Approximately400 calories |18g fat |50g carbohydrates |8g fiber |3g sugar |20g protein

LOW-CARB DINNER RECIPES

Grilled Chicken with Asparagus

Serving: One
Preparation Time: 10 minutes
Cooking Time: 10 minutes

Ingredients:
- 1 boneless, skinless chicken breast (about 6 oz)
- 1 cup asparagus, trimmed
- 1 tablespoon olive oil
- Salt and pepper to taste
- 1 teaspoon garlic powder

Preparation Method:

1. Preheat the grill to medium-high heat.

2. Drizzle chicken breast and asparagus with olive oil; season with salt, pepper, and garlic powder.

3. Grill chicken for about 5-6 minutes per side until cooked through.

4. Grill asparagus for about 4-5 minutes until tender.

Nutritional Value: Approximately 350 calories | 12g fat | 0g carbohydrates | 0g fiber | 0g sugar | 54g protein

Zucchini Lasagna

Serving: One
Preparation Time: 15 minutes
Cooking Time: 30 minutes

Ingredients:
- 2 medium zucchinis, sliced thinly
- 1 cup ricotta cheese
- 1 cup marinara sauce (sugar-free)
- 1 cup shredded mozzarella cheese
- 1/4 pound ground beef or turkey (optional)
- Salt and pepper to taste

Preparation Method:
1. Preheat the oven to 375°F (190°C).

2. If using, brown the ground meat in a skillet; drain excess fat.

3. In a baking dish, layer zucchini slices, ricotta cheese, marinara sauce, and ground meat if using.

4. Top with mozzarella cheese and season with salt and pepper.

5. Bake for about 30 minutes until bubbly and golden.

Nutritional Value: Approximately 400 calories | 25g fat | 12g carbohydrates |3g fiber|5g sugar|30g protein

Baked Salmon with Broccoli

Serving: One
Preparation Time: 5 minutes
Cooking Time: 20 minutes

Ingredients:
- 6 oz salmon fillet
- 1 cup broccoli florets
- 1 tablespoon olive oil
- Salt and pepper to taste
- Lemon wedges for serving (optional)

Preparation Method:

1. Preheat the oven to 400°F (200°C).

2. Place salmon on a baking sheet; drizzle with olive oil and season with salt and pepper.

3. Arrange broccoli around the salmon; drizzle with olive oil and season.

4. Bake for about 15-20 minutes until salmon is cooked through and flakes easily.

Nutritional Value: Approximately 450 calories |28g fat |0g carbohydrates |0g fiber |0g sugar |45g protein

Cauliflower Fried Rice

Serving: One
Preparation Time:10 minutes
Cooking Time:10 minutes

Ingredients:
- 2 cups cauliflower rice (fresh or frozen)
- 1/2 cup mixed vegetables (carrots, peas, bell peppers)
- 2 large eggs, beaten
- 2 tablespoons soy sauce or tamari
- 1 tablespoon sesame oil or olive oil

• Green onions for garnish (optional)

Preparation Method:

1. Heat oil in a skillet over medium heat; add mixed vegetables and sauté for about 3 minutes.

2. Push vegetables to one side; pour beaten eggs into the skillet and scramble until cooked.

3. Add cauliflower rice and soy sauce; stir-fry for about another 5 minutes until heated through.

Nutritional Value: Approximately 250 calories |15g fat |10g carbohydrates |4g fiber |3g sugar |12g protein

Stuffed Bell Peppers with Ground Turkey

Serving: One
Preparation Time: 15 minutes
Cooking Time: 30 minutes

Ingredients:
• 1 large bell pepper (any color)
• 1/2 pound ground turkey or beef
• 1/2 cup diced tomatoes (canned or fresh)
• 1/4 cup onion, diced
• 1 teaspoon Italian seasoning

●Salt and pepper to taste

Preparation Method:

1. Preheat oven to 375°F (190°C).

2. Cut the top off the bell pepper and remove seeds.

3. In a skillet, cook ground turkey with onion until browned; add diced tomatoes and seasoning.

4. Stuff the mixture into the bell pepper and place in a baking dish.

5. Bake for about 30 minutes until the pepper is tender.

Nutritional Value: Approximately 300 calories |15g fat |10g carbohydrates |3g fiber |5g sugar |30g protein

HIGH-CARB DESSERT RECIPES

Banana Oatmeal Cookies

Serving: One (approximately 2 cookies)
Preparation Time: 15 minutes
Cooking Time: 11-13 minutes

Ingredients:

- ½ cup unsalted butter, softened
- 1 cup packed light brown sugar
- 1 large egg
- ¾ cup mashed ripe bananas (about 2 medium)
- 1½ teaspoons pure vanilla extract
- 1 cup all-purpose flour
- 1 teaspoon baking soda
- 1 teaspoon salt
- 2 teaspoons ground cinnamon
- 3¼ cups old-fashioned oats
- 1 cup semi-sweet chocolate chips

Preparation Method:

1. Preheat oven to 350°F (175°C) and line baking sheets with parchment paper.
2. Cream together butter and brown sugar until light and fluffy.

3. Mix in the egg, mashed bananas, and vanilla until well combined.

4. In another bowl, whisk together flour, baking soda, salt, and cinnamon.

5. Gradually add dry ingredients to the wet mixture, then stir in oats and chocolate chips.

6. Scoop dough onto prepared sheets and bake for about 11-13 minutes until golden.

Nutritional Value: Approximately 200 calories | 10g fat | 30g carbohydrates | 2g fiber | 10g sugar | 3g protein

Sweet Potato Brownies

Serving: One (approximately one brownie)
Preparation Time: 15 minutes
Cooking Time: 25 minutes

Ingredients:
- 1 cup mashed sweet potatoes (about one medium)
- ½ cup almond flour
- ½ cup cocoa powder
- ½ cup maple syrup or honey
- 2 large eggs
- 1 teaspoon vanilla extract
- ¼ teaspoon salt
- ½ cup dark chocolate chips (optional)

Preparation Method:

1. Preheat oven to 350°F (175°C) and grease an 8x8-inch baking pan.

2. In a bowl, mix mashed sweet potatoes, almond flour, cocoa powder, maple syrup, eggs, vanilla, and salt until smooth.

3. Fold in chocolate chips if using.

4. Pour batter into the prepared pan and spread evenly.

5. Bake for about 25 minutes; let cool before cutting into squares.

Nutritional Value: Approximately 180 calories | 7g fat | 28g carbohydrates |4g fiber|10g sugar|3g protein

Quinoa Chocolate Chip Pudding

Serving: One
Preparation Time:10 minutes
Cooking Time: None (chill time required)

Ingredients:
- ½ cup cooked quinoa
- 1 cup almond milk (or milk of choice)
- 2 tablespoons cocoa powder
- 2 tablespoons maple syrup or honey
- ½ teaspoon vanilla extract

- ¼ cup chocolate chips (optional)

Preparation Method:

1. In a blender, combine cooked quinoa, almond milk, cocoa powder, maple syrup, and vanilla; blend until smooth.

2. Stir in chocolate chips if desired.

3. Chill in the refrigerator for at least an hour before serving.

Nutritional Value: Approximately250 calories |6g fat |45g carbohydrates |6g fiber |12g sugar |8g protein

Homemade Apple Pie

Serving: One slice
Preparation Time:20 minutes
Cooking Time:45 minutes

Ingredients:
- 1 pre-made pie crust (store-bought or homemade)
- 3 medium apples, peeled and sliced
- ¾ cup granulated sugar
- 1 tablespoon lemon juice
- 1 teaspoon cinnamon

●2 tablespoons butter, cut into small pieces

Preparation Method:

1. Preheat oven to 425°F (220°C).

2. In a bowl, toss apple slices with sugar, lemon juice, and cinnamon.

3. Place apple mixture in the pie crust; dot with butter.

4. Cover with another crust or lattice top; seal edges.

5. Bake for about 45 minutes until crust is golden and apples are tender.

Nutritional Value: Approximately300 calories |12g fat |45g carbohydrates |3g fiber |20g sugar |2g protein

Chocolate Lava Cake

Serving: One
Preparation Time:15 minutes
Cooking Time:12 minutes

Ingredients:

- ½ cup dark chocolate chips
- ¼ cup unsalted butter
- 2 large eggs
- ⅓ cup granulated sugar
- 2 tablespoons all-purpose flour
- Pinch of salt

Preparation Method:

1. Preheat oven to 425°F (220°C) and grease ramekins.

2. Melt chocolate chips and butter together in a microwave or double boiler; stir until smooth.

3. In a bowl, whisk eggs and sugar until thick; add melted chocolate mixture and mix well.

4. Fold in flour and salt until just combined.

5. Divide batter among ramekins; bake for about 12 minutes until edges are firm but center is soft.

Nutritional Value: Approximately 350 calories |22g fat |35g carbohydrates |2g fiber |20g sugar |6g protein.

LOW-CARB DESSERT RECIPES

Almond Flour Chocolate Chip Cookies

Serving: One (approximately 2 cookies)
Preparation Time: 10 minutes
Cooking Time: 12 minutes

Ingredients:
- 1/2 cup butter, softened
- 3/4 cup brown sugar or coconut sugar
- 1 large egg
- 2 teaspoons vanilla extract
- 3 cups blanched almond flour
- 1/2 teaspoon baking soda
- 1/2 teaspoon salt
- 1 1/4 cups chocolate chips (sugar-free)

Preparation Method:

1. Preheat the oven to 350°F (175°C) and line a baking sheet with parchment paper.

2. In a bowl, cream together the butter and sugar until light and fluffy.

3. Add the egg and vanilla, mixing until incorporated.

4. Mix in the baking soda and salt, then gradually add almond flour until combined.

5. Fold in chocolate chips.

6. Scoop dough onto the baking sheet about 2 inches apart and bake for about 11-13 minutes until golden brown.

Nutritional Value: Approximately 200 calories | 16g fat | 10g carbohydrates | 2g fiber | 5g sugar | 4g protein

Keto Cheesecake Bites

Serving: One (approximately two bites)
Preparation Time: 10 minutes
Cooking Time: None (chill time required)

Ingredients:
- 8 oz cream cheese, softened
- 1/4 cup powdered erythritol or other sweetener
- 1 teaspoon vanilla extract
- 1 large egg
- 1/4 cup almond flour (for crust)
- 1 tablespoon melted butter (for crust)

Preparation Method:

1. Preheat oven to 325°F (160°C).

2. Mix almond flour and melted butter; press into mini muffin tins for crusts.

3. Beat cream cheese, erythritol, vanilla, and egg until smooth.

4. Pour cheesecake mixture over crusts in muffin tins.

5. Bake for about 15-20 minutes until set; chill before serving.

Nutritional Value: Approximately 150 calories | 12g fat | 5g carbohydrates |0g fiber|3g sugar|4g protein

Sugar-Free Cheesecake

Serving: One (approximately one slice)
Preparation Time:15 minutes
Cooking Time:60 minutes

Ingredients:
- 16 oz cream cheese, softened
- 3/4 cup erythritol or preferred sweetener
- 3 large eggs
- 1 teaspoon vanilla extract

• 1 tablespoon lemon juice

Preparation Method:

1. Preheat oven to 325°F (160°C).

2. Beat cream cheese and erythritol until smooth; add eggs one at a time mixing well after each.

3. Stir in vanilla and lemon juice; pour into a greased springform pan.

4. Bake for about an hour; cool and refrigerate for at least four hours before serving.

Nutritional Value: Approximately 250 calories |20g fat |5g carbohydrates |0g fiber |2g sugar |6g protein

Fruit Sorbet

Serving: One
Preparation Time: 10 minutes
Cooking Time: None (freeze time required)

Ingredients:
• 1 cup frozen berries (strawberries, raspberries, or blueberries)
• 1 tablespoon erythritol or preferred sweetener
• 1 tablespoon lemon juice

Preparation Method:

1. In a blender or food processor, combine frozen berries, erythritol, and lemon juice.

2. Blend until smooth; taste and adjust sweetness if needed.

3. Transfer to a container and freeze for at least an hour before serving.

Nutritional Value: Approximately 100 calories |0g fat |25g carbohydrates |5g fiber |10g sugar |1g protein

Dark Chocolate Avocado Mousse

Serving: One
Preparation Time:10 minutes
Cooking Time: None

Ingredients:
- 1 ripe avocado
- 2 tablespoons unsweetened cocoa powder
- 2 tablespoons erythritol or preferred sweetener
- 1 teaspoon vanilla extract
- Pinch of salt

Preparation Method:

1. In a blender or food processor, combine avocado, cocoa powder, erythritol, vanilla extract, and salt.

2. Blend until smooth and creamy; taste and adjust sweetness if needed.

3. Chill in the refrigerator for about an hour before serving.

Nutritional Value: Approximately200 calories |15g fat |15g carbohydrates |7g fiber |2g sugar |3g protein

7-Day High-Carb Meal Plan

Day 1
Breakfast: Overnight Oats with Banana and Honey
Lunch: Quinoa and Black Bean Salad
Snack: Quinoa Energy Bites
Dinner: Lentil Soup with Whole Grain Bread
Dessert: Banana Oatmeal Cookies

Day 2
Breakfast: Whole Wheat Pancakes with Maple Syrup
Lunch: Sweet Potato and Chickpea Bowl
Snack: Sweet Potato Chips
Dinner: Quinoa and Veggie Salad
Dessert: Sweet Potato Brownies

Day 3
Breakfast: Whole Grain Pancakes with Banana
Lunch: Barley and Roasted Vegetable Soup
Snack: Oaty Apple Muffins
Dinner: Bean, Pea, and Lentil Salad
Dessert: Quinoa Chocolate Chip Pudding

Day 4
Breakfast: Quinoa Breakfast Bowl with Fruits
Lunch: Lentil and Vegetable Stir-Fry
Snack: Hummus with Whole Grain Pita
Dinner: Warm Lentil and Halloumi Salad

Dessert: Homemade Apple Pie

Day 5
Breakfast: French Toast with Cinnamon Apples
Lunch: Brown Rice and Grilled Chicken Bowl
Snack: Whole Grain Crackers with Hummus
Dinner: Spinach, Lentil, and Feta Bruschetta
Dessert: Chocolate Lava Cake

Day 6
Breakfast: Whole Grain Pancakes with Banana
Lunch: Sweet Potato and Chickpea Bowl
Snack: Quinoa Energy Bites
Dinner: Lentil Soup with Whole Grain Bread
Dessert: Sweet Potato Brownies

Day 7
Breakfast: Quinoa Breakfast Bowl with Fruits
Lunch: Barley and Roasted Vegetable Soup
Snack: Oaty Apple Muffins
Dinner: Quinoa and Veggie Salad
Dessert: Banana Oatmeal Cookies

7-Day Low-Carb Meal Plan

Day 1
Breakfast: Spinach and Goat Cheese Omelet
Lunch: Low-Carb Chicken Parmesan
Snack: Cucumber Slices with Guacamole
Dinner: Grilled Chicken with Asparagus
Dessert: Almond Flour Chocolate Chip Cookies

Day 2
Breakfast: Vegetable Scrambled Eggs
Lunch: Salmon Salad with Olive Oil
Snack: Hard-Boiled Eggs with Avocado
Dinner: Zucchini Lasagna
Dessert: Keto Cheesecake Bites

Day 3
Breakfast: Low-Carb Breakfast Casserole
Lunch: Broccoli and Cheese Frittata
Snack: Beef Jerky
Dinner: Baked Salmon with Broccoli
Dessert: Sugar-Free Cheesecake

Day 4
Breakfast: Smoked Salmon with Avocado
Lunch: Scrambled Eggs & Veggies
Snack: Cheese and Nut Plate
Dinner: Cauliflower Fried Rice
Dessert: Fruit Sorbet

Day 5
Breakfast: Keto Avocado Toast
Lunch: Steak Burrito Bowl
Snack: Celery Sticks with Peanut Butter
Dinner: Stuffed Bell Peppers with Ground Turkey
Dessert: Dark Chocolate Avocado Mousse

Day 6
Breakfast: Low-Carb Breakfast Casserole
Lunch: Low-Carb Chicken Parmesan
Snack: Beef Jerky
Dinner: Grilled Chicken with Asparagus
Dessert: Keto Cheesecake Bites

Day 7
Breakfast: Vegetable Scrambled Eggs
Lunch: Salmon Salad with Olive Oil
Snack: Cucumber Slices with Guacamole
Dinner: Baked Salmon with Broccoli
Dessert: Dark Chocolate Avocado Mousse

CONCLUSION

As men age, managing weight, energy, and muscle mass becomes increasingly challenging due to hormonal changes and metabolic slowdown. Carb cycling offers a dynamic, tailored approach to nutrition that can help men over 50 optimize their diet based on activity levels, body composition goals, and general health. By alternating between high-carb, low-carb, and no-carb days, this strategy encourages fat loss while preserving lean muscle, enhancing performance, and stabilizing blood sugar levels. The flexibility of carb cycling makes it easy to adapt to different lifestyles, fitness routines, and even medical conditions like diabetes or hypertension.

Men over 50 who incorporate carb cycling into their lives can experience better energy levels, more efficient fat-burning, and increased mental clarity. This dietary approach empowers you to make the most out of your workouts, while also promoting long-term health benefits like improved insulin sensitivity and hormonal balance.

Remember, the key to success with carb cycling is consistency and adaptation. As your body changes, your carb cycling plan can evolve to suit your needs.

Whether you're looking to lose weight, maintain muscle mass, or boost energy, carb cycling provides a sustainable, effective path forward. Now is the time to take control of your health and embrace the benefits of carb cycling. With discipline, patience, and this powerful approach, you can defy the limits of aging, regain your vitality, and achieve the fitness you deserve!

Made in the USA
Las Vegas, NV
01 March 2025

18908154R00056